A Feel Better Book

for Little
Tears

For our Dad, who is always sunshine on a cloudy day —HB & LB

To the reader, with sincerest hopes and best wishes that this book provides some tools in your toolbox to feel better in times of tears—SN-B

Books for Kids From the
American Psychological Association

MAGINATION PRESS is a registered trademark of the American Psychological Association. Order books here: maginationpress.org or 1-800-374-2721

Book design by Susan White
Printed by Lake Book Manufacturing, Inc., Melrose Park, IL

Library of Congress Cataloging-in-Publication Data
Names: Brochmann, Holly, author. | Bowen, Leah, author. | Ng-Benitez, Shirley, illustrator.
Title: A feel better book for little tears / by Holly Brochmann and Leah Bowen ;
    illustrated by Shirley Ng-Benitez.
Description: Washington, DC : Magination Press, an imprint of the American Psychological
    Association, [2019] | Summary: Illustrations and simple, rhyming text provide young children
    with tools for dealing with feelings of sadness, such as talking about what is wrong, crying,
    or doing something creative.
Identifiers: LCCN 2018030574 | ISBN 9781433830310 (hardcover) | ISBN 1433830310 (hardcover)
Subjects: | CYAC: Stories in rhyme. | Sadness—Fiction.
Classification: LCC PZ8.3.B779 Fd 2019 | DDC [E]—dc23 LC record available at
https://lccn.loc.gov/2018030574

Manufactured in the United States of America
10 9 8 7 6 5 4 3 2 1

A Feel Better Book

for Little Tears

by Holly Brochmann and Leah Bowen
illustrated by Shirley Ng-Benitez

MAGINATION PRESS · WASHINGTON', DC
American Psychological Association

My sweet little one,
you don't seem very cheery.
Are you feeling down,
and perhaps a bit dreary?

Maybe you're feeling
like nothing's alright.
Like the sky isn't blue
and the sun isn't bright.

There may be tears in your eyes
or an ache in your tummy.
You're moping around
and nothing seems funny.

If you don't feel like playing,
or even leaving your room,
then it sounds like the trouble
could be sadness and gloom.

Sadness is a feeling
that hurts way deep down.
It's the opposite of happy
and turns your smiles
into frowns.

Maybe you're missing someone,
or just having a bad day.
There could
be lots of
reasons
why you're
feeling
this way.

But there's good news, my friend.
You're not all alone!
And you don't have to deal with this
all on your own!

Sadness is normal.
You will make it through!
But while you are waiting
there are things you can do.

So when you are ready,
we can go at your pace,
and together we'll put
a smile back on your face!

We can start by just talking about why you feel sad. It may not be all better but it might not be as bad.

If you don't feel like talking,
instead you can try
just letting it out.
It's okay to cry!

So don't be
ashamed
if tears
start
to flow.
It can
actually
help
to let
feelings
show.

Next think of something
you like a whole lot.
Your favorite cartoon
or a new toy you just got.

Imagine playing with a puppy
or laughing with a friend.
Thinking happy thoughts
can help sadness mend.

You can also draw
a picture—
oh, the colors you will use!
A bright and sunny yellow
or rainy grays and blues.

Doing something creative
can help you start to heal.
A rainbow or a cloud,
just try drawing what you feel.

When you're in a gloomy mood
finding stuff to do
gives your thoughts a break,
and that can help, too.

Make a list of things,
we can write each one down.
Maybe sing your favorite song
or arrange your toys all around.

Let's bake a batch of cookies
or build a pillow fort.
Go outside to stretch your legs
and play your favorite sport!

It may not seem fun at first,
but after a little while
you might find you feel better...
is that a little smile?

If staying busy doesn't work,
let's try this instead.
Put your hands together
and place them on your head.

Now take a
deep breath in
slowly through
your nose.
Imagine air is flowing
from your head
down to your toes.

Blow it softly out
as gentle as you can.
Let your shoulders relax
while you slowly drop your hands.

Then pretend you are outside
and looking at the sky.
Watch the clouds float above
and the birds flying high.

Now let your breath move
like the swaying trees,
breathing in and out
slowly with the breeze.

If those smiles still don't come,
please just keep in mind,
you won't be sad forever!
It just might take some time.

So hang in there, little one.
Happy days are on the way!
The sun will shine again,
and everything will be okay!

Note to Parents and Caregivers

Of all the many human emotions, sadness can be one of the most difficult to manage. It occurs at many levels and in many different ways; it can be as simple as disappointment or as complex as grief and depression. Commonly identified as one of the primary or core emotions, sadness is also one of the first to develop and can be experienced very early in life. *A Feel Better Book for Little Tears* is a beginner's book that addresses the overall concept of sadness and gives parents and caregivers tools to not only help children process and cope with this difficult emotion, but to convey that it's normal—everyone feels sad sometimes. And even though sadness can be uncomfortable, for both the child and the caregiver, there is actually value in feeling sad. As stated by psychoanalyst Carl Jung, "The word 'happy' would lose its meaning if it were not balanced by sadness." There are happy times, but there will also be sad times, and this book aims to help our little ones work through those sad times and have hope that there will be sunny days ahead.

Responding to Sadness
There may be tears in your eyes, or an ache in your tummy.
Sadness can be felt in a variety of physical ways, including some that your child may not yet be able to communicate. They will likely learn early on that the obvious, universal sign for sadness is tears, but it can also manifest very differently and can be displayed more like anger, isolation, clinginess, or any number of other behaviors. First take note and be aware of changes in behavior that may demonstrate the less obvious reactions. Then you can help them connect those reactions to sadness with verbal cues. For example, if your child is being extra clingy, you can simply acknowledge their feelings by saying, "I know it makes you sad when Mommy can't be with you all the time."

There could be lots of reasons why you're feeling this way.
Children can be sad for so many reasons, some of which may be significant for the family (loss of a loved one, a best friend moving away, etc.) while others may seem minuscule and perhaps even ridiculous. But it's important to remember that while the child's feelings might appear insignificant to you as an adult, they are quite the opposite from the child's perspective. So bear in mind age-appropriate sadness. Rather than trivializing the child's feelings, instead respond with both empathy and sympathy. "I'm so sorry you can't wear your monster shirt today. I know it's your favorite and you are sad that it isn't clean. I understand how you feel, because I feel sad when that happens to me, too." Responding with empathy will allow your child to feel heard and understood.

Normalizing Sadness
You're not all alone! And you don't have to deal with this all on your own!
One of the most important messages you can convey to your child during times of sadness is that you are there for them. Sadness can be a lonely emotion, especially if experiencing something very personal and individual. However, it helps to have support from someone who knows what you are going through. If your child loses their favorite stuffed animal, for example, listen to them, however often they want to talk about it. Storytelling in this way may be their way to process their feelings. You may also normalize their feelings by sharing a story about how you experienced a similar loss when you were

their age. Be honest about how sad you were and how you cried. Talk about what helped you with your sad feelings or how you handled it. In the meantime, let them know you will be there for them if they need extra snuggles at night, extra hugs, or a shoulder to cry on.

It can actually help to let feelings show. Parents often try to be strong for their children, to show them that everything is going to be okay. However, it can actually be beneficial for a child to see adults showing appropriate emotion. It is okay to say, "Daddy is sad, too" or "Daddy misses him, too." This normalizes the child's sadness and demonstrates that these feelings are not something they need to try to mask or feel ashamed of. Furthermore, while the concept of "staying strong" is often encouraged in times of sadness, true strength and resilience is built by learning to process emotions, rather than ignoring them. Parents and caregivers should let the child experience and process the sadness; doing this, you are allowing them to grieve the loss, which is an essential first step in the healing process. By allowing those feelings to happen, your child is also learning that they are capable of coping with big emotions.

Coping With Sad Feelings
Doing something creative can help you start to heal.
Creative activities can be a wonderful outlet for expressing sad feelings in a constructive way. For example, your child can draw a picture of what they are sad about or what might make them feel happy. Perhaps they are at their father's house for the weekend and are missing their mother. Dad can suggest they draw a picture of themselves with their mom,

or they can draw a picture to give their mom. So rather than saying, "It's okay, don't be sad. I'm here," try saying, "I see you're missing your mom right now. Let's try drawing a picture of how you are feeling. Then you can give it to her when you see her tomorrow." Music, art projects, modeling clay—there are many ways to use creativity to help process emotions, so get creative!

Now let your breath move like the swaying trees, breathing in and out slowly with the breeze. Teaching mindfulness and relaxation at an early age helps set the stage for children to continue to use these practices throughout a lifetime, especially if they learn it's doable, enjoyable, and beneficial. Deep breathing is especially useful, as it increases the flow of oxygen and therefore slows the heartbeat, creating a physical sense of calm.

The visualization technique of picturing the trees swaying, the clouds softly moving by, and the ocean waves crashing gently in and out can also help a child (and caregiver!) feel more calm. And to continue with being creative, you can have the child draw their "happy place" when they are done with the visualization.

Doing these practices at the same time as your children helps the caregiver to remain calm as well. Dealing with a child's sadness can be both difficult and uncomfortable for a caregiver, so practicing these breathing techniques simultaneously can help both of you feel more at ease. Try practicing during calm moments, as well—this will build the skill set for the child to self-regulate later, in moments of higher emotions.

There's Hope!

You won't be sad forever, it just might take some time.

Some things just take time. Depending on what the child is sad about, they may never completely lose the sense of loss, but over time they can learn how to cope and feel happy again. On the other hand, the child may move on quite fast if the sadness is more minor. But either way, the main point to remember is that the child should be allowed to process their feelings at their own pace. There is no get-over-your-sadness timeline. And while it is quite tempting to try and take away your child's pain, in the long run, allowing your child to sit with the sadness, and hold that space, will help them learn at an early age that they are capable of getting through these tough feelings and rediscovering happiness on the other side.

A Final Thought

While this book is aimed at giving caregivers simple and effective tools to use at home, in school, or as a clinical supplement, a parent or caregiver should seek additional help if they feel it is necessary. It's important to note that while sadness is a natural emotion, excessive or prolonged depression or grief may require professional guidance. Your child's pediatrician can provide a list of licensed mental health professional referrals.

About the Authors

Sisters LEAH BOWEN and HOLLY BROCHMANN are dedicated wives, mothers, and authors, each passionate about contributing to a mentally healthier society in a meaningful way. Leah has a master of education degree in counseling with a focus in play therapy. She is a licensed professional counselor and registered play therapist in the state of Texas where she currently practices, and she is committed to helping her child clients work through issues including trauma, depression, and anxiety. Holly has a degree in journalism and enjoys creative writing both as a hobby and as a primary part of her career in public relations. This is the sisters' third book in the Feel Better Books for Little Kids series published by Magination Press. Both sisters live in Texas. Visit @bsistersbooks on Instagram and Twitter.

About the Illustrator

SHIRLEY NG-BENITEZ loves to draw! Nature, family, and fond memories of her youth inspire her mixed-media illustrations. Since '98, she's owned gabbyandco.com designing, illustrating, and lettering for the technology, greeting card, medical, toy, and publishing industries. She's living her dream, illustrating and writing picture books in San Martin, California, with her husband, daughters, pup, and two kittens. Shirley is honored to have illustrated this book as well as the other two books in the series, *A Feel Better Book for Little Worriers* and *A Feel Better Book for Little Tempers*, both also by Holly Brochmann and Leah Bowen and published by Magination Press. Visit shirleyngbenitez.com.

About Magination Press

MAGINATION PRESS is an imprint of the American Psychological Association, the largest scientific and professional organization representing psychologists in the United States and the largest association of psychologists worldwide.